QUALITIES
TO PRACTICE TODAY TO BE
SUCCESSFUL
IN LIFE!

Dr Bhoopalam Sunil

RIGI PUBLICATION

QUALITIES TO PRACTICE TODAY TO BE SUCCESSFUL IN LIFE!

By

Dr Bhoopalam Sunil

Copyright© Dr Bhoopalam Sunil 2021

Originally published in India

Printer: Deunique Printers

Edition:1

ISBN: 978-81-948315-6-3

Published by RIGI PUBLICATION

777, Street no.9, Krishna Nagar Khanna-141401 (Punjab), India

Website: www.rigipublication.com

Email: info@rigipublication.com

Phone: +91-9357710014, +91-9465468291

INTRODUCTION

Being successful in life is a goal that everybody wants to achieve. However, we can observe that not every person is successful or not everybody is happy with what they have achieved in their lives. Most of the people feel that their day-to-day life is full of regrets thinking about what they could have done right in the past. However, we need to remember that life is not about regrets.

Life is about learning from past mistakes and building a beautiful life in future. Everybody wants to be successful but is everyone willing to put in the amount of time and effort that is needed to be successful in life? If you ask a class filled with many students - *How many of you want to be successful in life?* you will probably see every hand in the class go up. But when you ask how many of them are willing to put in the time, efforts and patience to practice all the qualities that is needed to be successful in life, you will see them putting their hands down.

How can one be successful in life? Well, it depends on how success is defined by each person as success in itself varies from person to person and is highly subjective. What may be called as successful to one person might not be that of a great feat to another. However, on a general note, we can define that being successful in life means being happy and satisfied with professional and personal life. For starters, if you want to answer how to be successful in life, you should probably begin from looking at the qualities and the habits that are practiced by people who are deemed to be successful today globally.

If you closely look at the habits practiced by some of the most successful people in the world today, you will definitely see similar patterns. The difference between the ordinary people and the extra ordinary people is that little extra amount of time and efforts the successful people put in their lives to build a life they love and to have the most beautiful relationships both in their personal and professional lives.

This book is a compilation of the observations made about the qualities which needs to be practiced today for any person to be successful in life after having observed some of the most successful people from around the world. Read on and practice these habits in order to build the successful life that you always wanted to live. Remember that what's more important than reading this is putting these habits into practice. As a general rule, we all are aware that any habit takes about 90 days to become a Lifestyle. So, if you really want to be successful in life, follow these habits and inculcate them into your day-to-day life. Be motivated to make your dreams into reality and rest assured that your dream life is only a few steps away. Read on to discover the most important habits you should start practicing in your life in order to be successful!

ABOUT THE AUTHOR

Dr Bhoopalam Sunil

Bhoopalam Family is a well-known family in Shimoga, Bhoopalam Chandrashekariah was a great freedom fighter.

Bhoopalam Chandrashekariah was the General Secretary of VHP. His younger brother Bhoopalam Puttananjappa was a M.A. gold medalist and a leading lawyer in late 60s. Bhoopalam Puttananjappa's elder son was Bhoopalam Mahabala who was captain of YMCA Cricket team and president of the club 'The Bangalore City Institute". He was a leading textile merchant and partner of Tallam Nanjunda Setty. Bhoopalam Mahabala's eldest son was Bhoopalam Sunil born on 18-01-1967. Bhoopalam Sunil did his schooling in Baldwins & Valleys. Bhoopalam Sunil studied in National College. He completed B.A., B.B.A. and M.B.A.

Dr Bhoopalam Sunil is a reputed author, writer and a poet. His books crackling jocks for all and commonly confused words is published by JAICO and KINNARI Publications. His articles are published in Deccan Herald, Indian Express and several magazines.

Dr Bhoopalam Sunil established Gandhi Old Age Home in 2001 There are 125 inmates, who are old people. The inmates are given free food free accommodation, free clothes, free medicines and free insurance policies. Dr Bhoopalam Sunil mobilized funds for the buildings at Gandhi Old Age Home through Rotarys., Lions, Round Table and many other charitable institutions.

There are 18 staff people to look after them. The home is around 50,000 Sq.ft. Medical Education Minister Ramachandre Gowda had inaugurated a Ganapathi temple in Gandhi Old Age Home in the year 2014. Incidentally, Dr. Bhoopalam Sunil has received many awards to date. Some of them are

- Jai Prakash Narayan National Award
- Visweshwaraian Global Award for Excellence
- Aryabhatta Award
- Rajya Ratna Award
- Adarsha Ratha Award
- Karnataka Padmashree Award
- Environment Award

- Dr. Bhoopalam Sunil received Honarary doctorate in the year 2017.
- He is the chairman of Advisory board of Kannada T.V.
- He is the Vice President of Karnataka Arya Vyshya Sahithya Parishad.
- He is the Business development chairman of world Arya Vyshya Mahasabha.
- He is the vice president of Vasavi Temple Kothnur, Banasvadi.
- He is the chairman of Vasavi Raktha Chetana Trust.
- He is the Deputy Governer of Vasavi Clubs International.
- He is the Joint Secretary of Karnataka Arya Vyshya Maha Mandali.
- Dr Bhoopalam Sunil has interviewed many social dignitaries for

the magazine Environment Pollution, where he is the sub-editor.

- He has interviewed Joint Commissioner of GST Pratap Kumar and Gopinath Commissioner Income tax.

DEDICATION

I Dr Bhoopalam Sunil dedicate this book to my parents.
Bhoopalam Suvarna and B P Mahabala

Author's family

(In the photo)

Dr Bhoopalam Sunil, Prem Kumar, Baby Ritanya

Shruthika, Sunitha and Suyog

Shri Sadananda Gowda central minister for chemicals and fertilizers released stamps on Gandhi Old Age Home and Dr Bhoopalam Sunil

TABLE OF CONTENTS

1. STRONG AND POWERFUL BELIEF — 13

2. GENUINE EFFORTS — 19

3. PERSISTENCE — 21

4. DEDICATION — 25

5. COMMITMENT — 28

6. GRATITUDE — 31

7. POSITIVE ATTITUDE — 34

8. ACTION ORIENTED, BEING A DOER — 38

9. STRATEGIC PLANNING — 42

10. INNOVATION AND CEATIVITY — 46

11. VALUE FOR TIME AND TIME MANAGEMENT — 52

12. STRESS AND CRISES MANAGEMENT — 57

13. THE RIGHT BELIEF SYSTEMS — 63

14. GET OUT OF THE BLAME GAME — 70

15. BUILD GREAT PERSONAL RELATIONSHIPS — 78

16. CHASE YOUR DREAMS — 85

17. TAKE FULL OWNERSHIP OF YOUR LIFE! — 92

CHAPTER 1 - STRONG AND POWERFUL BELIEF

Belief systems can often make or break you. It is not an understatement when people say that what you believe is what you are and what you believe is what you become. It is also not false when people say that if you believe in yourself, then God will believe in you. Such is the power of a strong and empowering belief system. How you think determines to a great deal about what you decide to do and ultimately the kind of life that you will have. If you believe that you are weak, weak you shall be. If you believe that you are strong, strong you shall be.

In Mahatma Gandhiji's quote - "*Man often becomes what he believes himself to be. If I keep on saying to myself that I cannot do a certain thing, it is possible that I may end up by really becoming incapable of doing it. On the contrary, if I shall have the belief that I can do it, I shall surely acquire the capacity to do it, even if I may not have it at the beginning*". This quote alone told by the father of the nation has the power to change the belief system of any person. Belief systems are less about what the society has taught you and more about what you think of yourself and how much trust and faith you have in your

own abilities. At the end of the day, only you can decide what you can or cannot do.

So you must be wondering what are some of the most powerful and empowering belief systems one can have. Here are some of the most powerful beliefs you need to have about yourself in order to create miracles in your life and do great things. Remember that your best life is only one decision away and that you can absolutely create the life you want for yourself. Do not let anyone else steer your life and lead your life according to how you want your life to be. For starters, read on some of the most powerful beliefs you need to have. Start believing them for real and make them a part of your internal dictionary. Read on:

- **I am enough** - It is very sad that most people believe that they are not worthy, not enough and want to prove their worth to the world by building a beautiful home, buying a luxurious car, running a successful business or having the perfect body shape. While it is good to have goals and ambition in life, it is also important to not beat yourself up because you are trying to be the best or perfect at everything. In reality, nobody is perfect.

Each person who is successful started small and started with the belief of *I am enough*. You will learn things as you start doing them but the belief that you are not enough is a limiting belief and it will stop you from even trying things. And without trying, how can you ever achieve anything in your life?

- **I can do this!** - The world and the people around you can tell you a hundred reasons on why you cannot do something. However, you should be the ultimate controller of your life and what matters the most is not what people think about your capabilities but what you think about your own capabilities. Start replacing your *I cannot do this* to *I can do this* and you will see yourself changing for the good. Believing you can do something is a strong and powerful belief which makes you chase things, which makes you want to try and explore new waters and ultimately which makes you a champion at everything that you want to to excel in. It is not false when people say that for a willing heart moving mountains is also not a difficult task. It is true that where there is a will there is a way. ***Start believing that you can do things and you certainly will one day!***

- **I take full responsibility of my life** - Taking responsibility of your life means that you take charge of your life and genuinely believe that it is you who is responsible for the lifestyle that you're having, for the income that you're earning, for the quality of your relationships and everything in between. Taking charge of your life makes you the ultimate master of your life and you stop being the one who complains and turning into a person who takes actions instead of being a mere spectator. You will notice that your life will change for the

good when you start taking responsibility of your life. Blaming others for what is going wrong in your life is very easy. It is something most normal people can do and mostly will do. However, if what you want for yourself is an extra ordinary life, it is important for you to take full and complete responsibility of your life. If something is going wrong in your life, instead of complaining and blaming others, you should think about how you can change the situation and what you can do in order to bring a positive outcome. This is applicable in every walk of your life.

• **I can learn as I go along** - Many people have a syndrome called the perfectionist syndrome. The perfectionist syndrome is believing that you are not ready even after having adequate evidence that you do have the skills and abilities that is needed to complete a particular job. After interviewing hundreds of successful people, it was found out that most of the people who are successful still believe that they do not have the necessary skills that was needed for them to be successful.

On the contrary, the world perceive them to be successful. Now stop and think - Have you been a victim of the imposter syndrome? Do you feel you are not enough? Do you feel you are not ready? Do you feel you need a hundred more skills and abilities to be able to do something? If your answers to these questions are **yes** - then be reminded that you are more likely to feel the same way for many more years to come and you will never actually get started with doing anything. Thus, it is important for you to believe that you know enough to get started and you will figure out the rest of the things as the path unfolds. Nobody was born an expert and expertise is something that comes after experience. How will you ever be able to gain experience without starting to do? ***Believe and truly believe that you will learn as you go along.***

• **I have an infinite potential inside of me** - As mentioned earlier, your belief system are what defines who you are and what you will do. Believing that you are unfit to do anything is disempowering enough to not let you even get started with whatever that you want to do. On the other hand, believing that you have an infinite potential inside of you allows you to start and grow as you you take on the journey of being successful. Now, it is true that you will find people around you, even the closest circle to tell you that you are not worthy or that you are not enough. However, remember that it is not what others believe about you which defines what you can or cannot do but your beliefs of yourself. Remember that you are enough. Remember that you are worthy. ***Remember and truly believe in The infinite potential that you have inside of you.***

- **I know how to deal with tough people and tough situations** - Nobody in this world is immune to tough people or tough situations. The most successful people have also gone through the darkest of times. Remember that every cloud has a silver lining and that every situation also has something good coming after it. Believing that you know how to deal with tough people and tough situations is an empowering belief which will make the journey less painful and which will let you see the situation through the eyes of a person who is looking for opportunities. You cannot avoid tough people and tough situations. You can choose and control how you react to tough people and tough situations.

- **Nothing can break my heart or ruin my life** - Remember that nothing in life is important enough to ruin or break your life. Do not let your relationships or career and other materialistic things in your life affect how you feel about yourself and your life. Do not let anybody tell you what you cannot do. It is you and only you who can decide what you can and cannot do in your life. Give the full responsibility of breaking your heart only to yourself.

- **I can create the miracles I want to see happen in my life** - All of you are taught to wait for the angel to save us from our problems. As we grow up, we realise that there are no angels and there is no santa claus. There is no Prince charming who will come and comfort the damsel in distress that you are. Bottomline - the takeaway is that do not be a damsel in distress. Instead, be the king or the queen who has full control over your life and truly believe that you can create the miracle that you want to create for you.

God is always there to look after what happening in your life and to guide you in the light but the ultimate steps need to be taken by you. Miracles are possible and remember that you are the creator of miracles in your life. Believe in the creator. Believe in The infinite potential God has given you and be the creator of miracle that you want to see in your life!

These are some of the strong and empowering beliefs most of the successful people carry in their minds which has truly bought them a long way. Remember that your beliefs define and design your life. ***Take charge of what you believe and change your realities!***

CHAPTER 2 - GENUINE EFFORTS

There used to be a time where children were taught that *hard work is the key to success.* Nowadays, this age old proverb has been replaced by *smart work is the key to success.* So what really is the key to success?

Ask successful people and you would know that they genuinely believe that true efforts, clarity and direction are the keys to success. There is no substitute for effort. Genuine efforts are super important in any walk of your life to get ahead and to perform better in every single aspect of life.

However, you can note that genuine efforts is seriously underrated these days and people believe that genuine efforts are not to be put by humans but by donkeys. It is time that people understand that even when the culture suggested that smart work is the key to success, work was still an integral part. *Smart work does not mean no work.*

The younger generations especially have got this wrong and that is the reason you see many youngsters not hustling, not grinding, and not chasing things that they want. Dreams are to be pursued. Relationships are to be pursued. Career is to be pursued. Everything that you want in your life if is to be pursued. Period.

Expecting results without putting in the needed efforts is the most foolish thing one can do with their lives. Be it any walk of life, from your personal relationships to your professional career - putting in the needed amount of time and efforts into them is detrimental in determining how successful you will be. And where does the will of putting in genuine efforts come from? The biggest motivation to putting in genuine efforts is the will to do it.

In other words, if you do not have the will to do something you better not pursue it because you are not going to put in the efforts or the time that is needed to do it and thus, it is surely going to be an unsuccessful endeavour. No matter what you do, you can never beat the importance of genuine efforts in making anything happen. Rome was not built in a day. Nothing can be built in a day. Everything worthy of creation takes time and efforts.

So, if you want anything in your life, the first thing you need to understand is that you will be needed to put in the required genuine efforts into it. Remember that nothing worth it comes free of cost. Everything has a price and you need to pay the price to get anything that you want.

Be willing to put in the needed efforts and the time to achieve whatever that you want from your life! Do not make the mistake of thinking that you will be able to create a beautiful life without being ready to put in the needed efforts. One of the most renowned motivational speakers Gary vaynerchuk says *"**Without hustle, your talent will only get you so far**"*. With that, remember that in order to go a long way in your life, be prepared and fall in love with putting in genuine efforts and to Hustle.

CHAPTER 3 - PERSISTENCE

Persistence is definitely one of the most charming and admirable attributes a person may have. Being persistent means that having the will to continue doing something until one achieves success without caring about the setbacks and failures that come along. More often than not, most people give up on their dreams and goals at the face of a couple of failures.

One needs to note that success is not something that comes on day 1 or day 2. It takes time for one to be successful and for anybody to master any skill or ability that makes them worthy in the first place to become successful. Thus, being persistent and consistent with the effort that you are putting in is very important. Being persistent is especially important in today's time where people have a hundreds of career paths to choose from.

Everything has become very easy to obtain these days with the advent of the internet and technology. Thus, people have become victims of consistently changing their goals and career paths. While it's not suggested that you stick to one on one goal throughout your entire life, it is also not suggested to keep changing your goals very frequently.

Failing again and again at something is what makes you stronger. Learning from your failures is the best way to move ahead and that is the only way to really master any skill or talent. Being jack of all trades and master of none will definitely lead you towards an ordinary life. But if you want to need an extra ordinary life and want to have extra ordinary experiences, persistence is one of the qualities you need to incorporate in your day to day life.

Be persistent in whatever that you do. Give yourself some time to get good at something. Do not expect results at the face of one or two trials. Remember that it is okay to fail and what's more important than succeeding at first shot is to be persistent and consistent in whatever that you are doing. Here are some simple steps on how to be persistent in your everyday life.

Simple tips on how to be persistent in your everyday life:

#1 - Define your goals and objectives

The first and foremost thing you need to do is to define your goals and objectives. It might sound astounding but it is true that many people do not have set goals and expectations from their lives. Remember that you will not get anything that you want from your life without planning for it or without wanting to have it in the first place. So stop being a person who looks at other's success and dreams to be successful one day without having goals and objectives.

Take time for yourself and truly ask yourself what is it that you want from your life. Write down your goals and objectives. This could be a five year plan or a three year plan or even an annual plan. What is important here is that you are defining what you want from your life so that you have something to pursue in the first place.

#2 - Define the WHY behind doing anything

After you have defined your goals and objectives, the next step would be to define why you want to achieve these things. Finding answers to your why could become the biggest motivation at times when you feel demotivated. Your voice should be strong enough to push you in your darkest times and to help you be persistent with whatever that you are pursuing.

For example, let's say you want to be a serial entrepreneur. Before going ahead with defining your action plan, think about *why* do you want to be a serial entrepreneur. What is it that can really motivate and drive you to chase your dream of being a serial entrepreneur. Write down and remember the why behind everything that you are pursuing. This will become the biggest source of inspiration that will fuel you when you do not feel driven towards your goals.

#3 - Think about the three or four biggest motivational drives for you

Motivational drives is very subjective and varies from person to person. What might motivate someone might fail to motivate someone else. Your motivational drives are specific to you. So think about the three or four biggest motivational drives. Everytime you feel down or feel demotivated or just having a bad day, think about these three to four biggest motivational drives and you will be pumped up to get at whatever that you want to pursue. Make this big motivational drives as your guiding forces to be persistent. ***Remember that giving up is easy, however holding on is what makes successful people successful.***

#4 - Celebrate the little victories that you have on your way

Most people forget to celebrate the little victories that they have achieved. As little children, we are all constantly motivated and appreciated by our parents or teachers when we have accomplished or achieved certain things. As we grow up, in the guise of being adults, we forget to celebrate the small victories that we have. We will not find people who will pat our backs.

So you should be the one who will pat your own back when you had little victories. These little celebrations are like your rewards for getting a few steps closer to your dream. Such celebrations and victories can be looked back upon at times when you feel demotivated or derailed and *that* helps you to be persistent.

CHAPTER 4 - DEDICATION

Stop for a moment and think about the last time you gave everything that you had in order for something to happen? When was the last time you really got carried away in something that you were doing and did not know how time passed? Don't you feel happy when you think about it? Where does real happiness come from?

Yes you guessed that right. Real happiness comes from a feeling that you have put in lots of quality time and dedication into doing something to an extent that you did not even realise how time passed by. That is what true dedication is all about. Dedication means that becoming so passionate about something that you tend to obsess over it and can't realise how time passes.

Being 100% committed and dedicated towards your goal has the infinite potential of making your dream or goal come true. If you are not dedicated in whatever that you are doing, you will probably struggle your way through to complete it and the end result will not be the one that will make you happy anyway.

Thus, if you are pursuing something that you are not happy doing, the first thing you will realise is that you are not putting or feeling a sense of dedication towards this work. Remember that without dedication

you will always struggle and ultimate results will also so not be up to the mark.

On the other hand, if you invest the same amount of time and energy is in the work that you are actually passionate about and can put into dedication, you can do wonders for yourself and your outcome will put you on cloud nine. So being really dedicated towards something comes down to the question - What is it that you feel extremely passionate about into which you can put in 100% dedication and commitment?

Here are some ways through which you can put in 100% dedication into whatever that you are doing:

#1 - Ask yourself if you really like what you're doing

The first step towards ensuring that you can put in 100% dedication into your work is to ask yourself - *if you really like what you are doing.* Ask yourself if you really enjoy what you are doing and if you really want to have the outcome that you are chasing. Nothing can beat true passion and love for doing something.

As a matter of fact, If you really love something that you are doing, dedication will make its way through in. Sachin tendulkar is devoted and dedicated towards playing cricket because he genuinely enjoys playing cricket and is genuinely passionate about the sport. So before thinking about putting in in your 100% or full dedication, be clear on what you are doing and if you really love whatever you are doing.

#2 - Remind yourself of your goals and objectives

it is easy for us to get distracted and to forget about the goals and objectives that we have set for ourselves. Write down your goals and objectives big and bold. Every time you feel let down, every time you feel unlucky, every time you find yourself complaining, every time you feel down - look at these goals and objectives and pump yourself. Be a constant reminder for yourself about your own goals and objectives and keep chasing them.

#3 - Ensure that you put in adequate efforts and time

Putting in adequate efforts and time cannot be replaced by anything else. If you want to become a master at something, you need to put in the needed and genuine efforts. Dedication comes through practice and involvement. Ask yourself from time to time and really look into what you are doing every day in order to reach your goal or objective. Do everything you can in order to ensure that you are on track and are on the path of chasing your dreams and goals. Something as simple as setting reminders in your phone can come a long way in determining your success and to remind you to be on track.

CHAPTER 5 - COMMITMENT

Have you noticed that some of the most successful people in the world are always committed to the work they do? If you have spent your time with some successful people, you might have noticed them say things like "I am sorry I cannot make it to the meeting because I have other prior commitments" Commitment is a quality that is found in successful people and it is definitely an ingredient to determine a person's success. If you are not committed towards anything in your life, the chances are that you will end up achieving nothing in life and it will be too late by the time you realise it.

Commitment is a quality that sets extra ordinary people apart from the ordinary people. So, what is commitment? Commitment is a pledge that obligates a certain person towards his goals or objectives. The reason commitments are so powerful is because they provide the inner motivation that is required in order to take actions towards achieving goals. Without commitment, it is very hard to to take actions towards goals and thus, it is very hard to be successful in life, or to have a successful relationship, successful business or achieve success in any other aspect of life.

While the first step is to have a certain set of goals and ambition in life, the second step is to have commitment towards it and live up to those commitments. The toughest part however is to be committed towards something consistently. Here are some things that you can do today in order to be committed towards anything consistently. Remember that commitment without consistency is going to lead you nowhere.

#1 - Make a list of the things that you want to accomplish

As simple as it may sound, many people do not have the habit of making a list of things that you want to accomplish in a particular week, month, or even a year. Without making lists and without knowing what is it that you exactly want to accomplish in a week, it is very difficult for you to keep up with the tasks that are needed to be done in order to accomplish those goals. Making lists are a powerful way of ensuring that you are keeping up with the actions that you want to take in a certain period of time.

TO DO LIST

For example: If you have a a goal of losing weight in 3 months, you need to make a list of the things that you are needed to do in order to lose weight in 3 months. This list must include everything from what you intend to eat and the kind of exercises that you wish to do. It must then be followed by the time schedule where you want to do these things. The next step is to simply stick to these actions and get the result that you desire.

#2 - Follow through the actions and the lists

Making list and defining the action plan is the first step but it is not all. The next most important step is to ensure that you stick to these actions and that is where your commitment comes into picture. You must follow through these actions and ensure that you do them every single day until you have accomplished your goals. Having a simple reminder application or a to-do list application will be very useful in this regard and will help you keep on track.

#3 - Prioritize your goals

As an individual, you might have different types of goals to be achieved in different aspects of life like relationships, friendships, business, hobbies and so on. However, it is important that you prioritise your goals so that you do not get to scattered away in the guise of achieving all your goals at the same time. Prioritise your goals and determine what goals that you want to accomplish faster than the others, and dedicate your energies and actions towards these goals first.

These are the three simple steps that you can take today to ensure that you are committed towards your goals. Remember that when it comes to commitment, the most important thing is to be consistent with everything that you do. Being committed towards anything for a small period of time is not going to yield you results in the long run.

CHAPTER 6 - GRATITUDE

Gratitude is a very powerful emotion which makes people happy, feel empowered and stronger. While it is very easy to complain about the things that you do not have in life, only some people can actually be thankful for the things that they have and be grateful about these little things. Gratitude is a quality that is practised by successful people and it should be practiced by anybody who wants to feel happy and contented in their life. A lack of gratitude often leads to unhappiness in life and regardless of how successful a person actually is in other aspects of life, he or she will not be able to feel happy about the things that they have accomplished. The beautiful thing about gratitude is that you cannot feel sorry for yourself or feel victimised when you are being grateful for the things that you have in your life.

Gratitude, in simplest of the terms is being thankful for the things that one has in life. Here are some simple ways through which you can develop gratitude in your day-to-day life and lead a more happy and contented life:

• Keep a gratitude journal in which you record everything that you are grateful for before you sleep. This is a great way of reminding you how lucky you are just before you sleep. This not only helps you develop the quality of gratefulness in your life but also helps induce better sleep.

• Express love and affection towards your loved ones on a regular basis and do this consciously. It is very easy for many people to take relationships, especially with loved ones for granted, and most of us never take the time to express love to our loved ones. A large part of practicing gratitude is to tell your loved ones just how much you love and appreciate them, and show them your affection.

• Include an act of kindness in your everyday life. Even though it might seem a little difficult to do it on an everyday basis, try to include at least some simple acts of kindness everyday in your life. It could be as simple as feeding a stray cat or dog.

• Notice the beauty in the nature and smile more often. We often forget how beautiful our nature is, and rarely do we take the time to actually just observe and enjoy the beauty of nature around us. Start doing this on every day basis and you will see a difference in the the emotions that you feel throughout the day.

• Nurture the relationships that you have. Be thankful for the friendships that have come along and tell your friends you love them. Tell your parents you love them. If you're missing someone, tell them. If you want to ask someone out for a party or a fun adventure, ask them.

• Watch inspiring positive videos that will remind you of the good that is left in the world. We are often mostly very attracted to the negative media, and the news that is spreading around the world about how bad and dangerous world can be. While it is true that world is not always a safe place to live in, we should understand that we need to make best of what we have and have the best time while we live here.

• Care for the people around you. Although at the outlook, we all try to care for the people around us, most of us end up failing at it without even realising it. Caring for the dependents at home is different from caring for the people who are aged or for the people in the community who are serving you everyday, like the janitors, cleaners, bus drivers and so on. Care for them and ask them how they're doing every now and then.

• Make a gratitude collage. This is a great way of reminding yourself everyday about the things that you are really very grateful for. Cut out the pictures of things you really love in your life and make a collage out of it, and stick it onto a place where you can see them everyday.

CHAPTER 7 - POSITIVE ATTITUDE

Mind is a very powerful place. What we think, we become. How we think about ourselves often reflects in our results and all action plans that follow. Having a positive attitude in life is very important to be successful. Without a positive outlook on life, one might get caught up in the harsh humdrum realities of life which might bring one's spirits down. One of the top qualities practiced by successful people is to have a positive attitude. There may be a hundred things to complain about everyday, but finding those few things which makes life positive and happy is very important. In the end, it is true that - life is not about what happens to you, it is about how you react to what happens to you. Healthy, positive attitude is very important to have a happy, contended and a successful life. There are many ways to develop your positive attitude. Here are a few very simple ways through which you can practice having positive attitude.

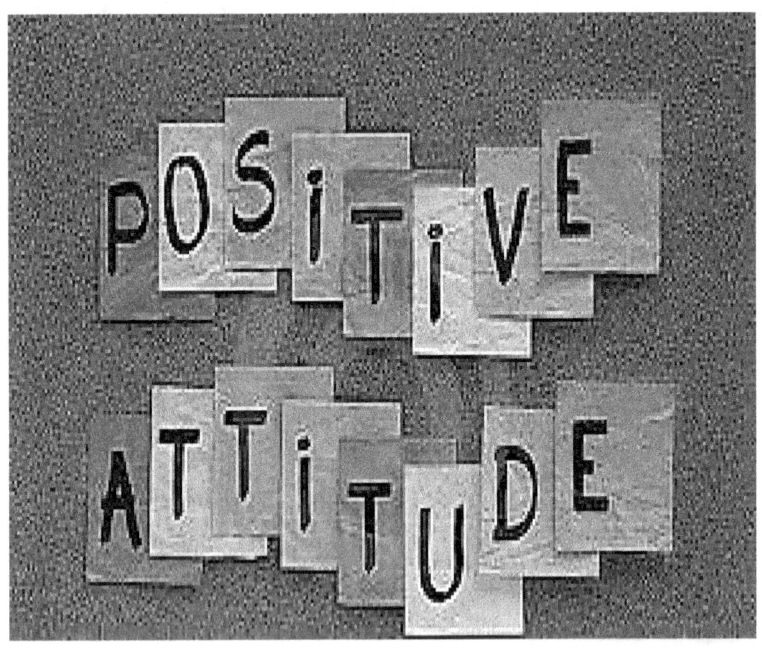

#1 - Be mindful about the internal dialogue that you have with yourself

When you have a negative thought about something, turn it around and make it into a positive one immediately. For example, if your mind says you cannot do something, turn it around and tell yourself that you can do it and even if you won't get it right the first time, you will try and get it right eventually. Be very mindful about internal dialogue that you have with yourself because at the end of the day, nobody can motivate you better than yourself.

#2 - Interact with positive environments and hang out with positive people

It is true that you are the average of the five people you hangout with. The kind of people you surround yourself with determines your mindset towards life to a large extent, and thus you should ensure that you only hang out with people who reinforce the good in you and help you bring out the best version of yourself. Never feel that you should hang out with people who you don't like to surround yourself with. Learn to say no to people. Being very mindful of the environment that you are surrounding yourself with is for your good and is going to benefit you in the long run in many ways.

#3 - Develop optimistic belief systems

Optimistic belief systems are beliefs that are pro-life and that have a positive outlook towards life overall. They are strong and empowering. They become the guiding principles at times when your energies are down and they drive you. Optimistic belief systems believe in the possibilities. They are the genesis of hope and they help you to keep marching forwards. Regardless of how hard things might get in your life, having an optimistic thinking will help you stay afloat and eventually figure out a way through which you will get out of your problems in life.

#4 - Get pleasure out of the simple things in life

In the busy routine that we all run, we often forget to derive pleasure out of the simple things in life. We do not need fancy vacations for fancy getaways in order to feel happy. Smallest of the things like making someone laugh or feeding a stray cat or dog or watering your plants can make you feel happy and change your mood. Do not underestimate the power of laughing. Find things around you that makes you happy and indulge in passions and hobbies that genuinely make you feel alive. This will help you develop an overall positive attitude in your life.

#5 - Allow yourself to be loved

Many of us are too hard on ourselves and do not let others to fully express their love and affection towards us. This is a negative attitude towards life and we must take conscious actions to beat this attitude. You are worthy of real love and affection, and you should let others to love you in whatever ways they can. Do not live in your shell and do not have too many walls around you stopping you from making genuine connections with people around you.

#6 - Listen to motivational podcasts

There are many beautiful podcasts run by some of the most influential motivational speakers out there and you should subscribe to some of those and try to listen to them from time to time. Such motivational podcasts will help you develop gratitude in life and have an overall positive attitude towards life. Besides, having someone who will constantly push you to think positively might be very useful in actually helping you to think positively.

Remember these beautiful lines by Walter D. Wintle to help you keep going and have a positive attitude in life:

If you think you are beaten, you are;

If you think you dare not, you don't;

If you want to win but think you can't;

It's almost a cinch you won't.

If you think you'll lose, you're lost;

For out of the world we find

Success begins with a person's will;

It's all in a state of mind.

Life's battles don't always go

To the stronger and faster human,

But sooner or later the people who win

Are the ones who think they can.

CHAPTER 8 – ACTION ORIENTED, BEING A DOER

Many of us want to do a lot of things but end up *almost* doing them. Having a long list of to-dos won't help in actually doing them. Thinking about doing things and actually doing things are two different things. While many people keep thinking about doing, only successful people actually do things and get the desired results from their work.

This is a quality of successful people. They are DOERS. They aren't the ones who talk about doing great things, they chase their dreams and put in efforts and practice to bringing their dreams to reality. If you want to be successful in any aspect of life - you cannot ignore just how important it is to be a doer and take action towards your goals. Have you been taking actions towards your goal? When was the last time you took an active action towards making your dreams come true? Here are a few quick practical tips that'll help you become an action oriented person who DOES what he or she says. Use them effectively to change your habits and finally get to doing things in order to drive results rather than talk or complain about the same problems.

#1 - Know what you CAN control and what you CANNOT

There are only so things which are actually in our control, like the time we set apart for doing something, the motivation we have in order to do something, our own energies and perceptions. However, many external factors like what others are doing, the weather, the economy, the past, others' opinions etc are not in our control. We cannot change them regardless of how hard we try to change them. Thus, the first step towards being an action-oriented person is to understand that there are certain things which are beyond our control. Thus, worrying about them will do no good. Instead, taking action on what things we can control brings us closer to success. For example: Instead of cribbing about the bad climate for having no motivation to work, you can decide to take a nap for some time and get back to work.

#2 - Don't wait for a perfect timing

There is no PERFECT timing to do anything. It is just another myth we tell ourselves to delay a task or a project or a deadline. There are many people who die doing nothing because they waited too long for a "perfect" timing. Remove such ideologies from your mind and truly understand that, the perfect timing is when you sit to do something. Been putting off something for far too long? Do it within the next week. Waiting for something that does not exist is silly and won't take you anywhere.

#3 - Reward yourself every time you check something off your list

Sometimes, all we need is a little motivation in order to get some things done. This motivation could be different factors for different people. What is yours? Would a ice cream treat for yourself motivate you enough to get something done? Define what will push you to do something and complete a particular task and reward yourself when you accomplish it. Rewarding yourself is a great way to keep you going and enjoy the journey too.

#4 - Surround yourself with people who are doers

Tell me who your friends are, I'll tell you who you are. You have probably heard this proverb somewhere. It is true for everyone. Observe the close circle friends of highly successful people. You'll notice that successful people always try to surround themselves with like-minded and positive people who do not pull them down but try to push them forward. That's the kind of friends circle everyone deserves. If you have been surrounded with toxic people for whatever reasons, this is the time to cut them off your lives. Surround yourself with friends who motivate you and who are doers themselves.

#5 - Be willing to fail

Many people don't start doing certain tasks be ayse they have this huge fear of failure. Fear of failure has killed more dreams than the failure itself. Not willing to fail is a sign that one can never succeed. Successful people didn't just "get lucky" and achieve success overnight. They've succeeded because of the consistent efforts that they've put in and the long hours that they've dedicated in order to achieve something. Similarly, they're also people who are okay with failing. Failures are great learning opportunities. It is okay to fail. It is okay to make mistakes. The key takeaway is to keep learning from your experiences and marching forward. If you've done so much, that must be more than sufficient to help you keep going.

CHAPTER 9 – STRATEGIC PLANNING

There are many different opinions on how one can achieve success, happiness, fulfillment and joy in life. Planning is one of the most integral parts of achieving success in anything in one's life. Whether it is wealth creation, happiness, healthy relationships, healthy body or a big business that you are chasing - planning is a must to achieve any of this. In fact, planning is the first step one needs to take in order to achieve anything in life.

If you ask a group of people about what they want to achieve in their lives, you'll get varied answers from them. A few of them would be:

- I want to make more money
- I want to build healthy relationships
- I want to travel the world
- I want to build a bigger house and buy a better car
- I want to build a successful business
- I want to be a great polician
- I want to lose weight
- I want to be respected

All these goals are worthwhile to pursue. However, if you ask same bunch of people if they have any roadmap that they have defined in order to achieve the goals, most of them would have no answer. Planning sets successful people apart from unsuccessful ones. Unsuccessful people dream a lot but never draw a concise plan that'll be needed in order to make these dreams come true. Successful people on the other hand devise strategic plans to achieve their goals, stick to these action plans and live the kind of life they want.

The list of dreams is a big one. The list goes on and on and it varies from one person to another. Whatever your goals are, strategic planning is one of the key steps involved in order to achieve them. Here is why strategic planning is so important for everyone and why it is important for you to devise a concrete plan to achieve your goals right away:

#1 - Planning helps you identify what is important to you

While many people like to think that they know exactly just what they want from their lives, the truth is far from this thinking. Most people are rather confused about what they want from their life which acts as the biggest obstacle that'll keep them from achieving things in life. When you choose to plan your life, it helps you to identify what is most important to you. This clarity will give a sense of direction in your life and you'll start getting closer and closer to achieving and living your dream life.

#2 - Planning provides you with a roadmap to success

Planning gives you a clear picture of the things you want and also helps you understand what actions you need to take right now to get closer to your dreams. It is a roadmap that'll keep you on the right track. It not only tells you what you should or shouldn't be doing, but also keeps you away from wastage of time that you may do in case you don't have any plan in place. It'll keep you from doing wasteful activities that won't add any value in your life and which won't take you any closer to your dreams.

#3 - Planning your life gives you an immense control over your life

When you strategically plan about the things you want in your life, you won't be wasting your time in thinking about wasteful or unfulfilling tasks and activities. It will help you stay focused and stick to a plan instead of wandering about and leaving things to chance. Besides, it also helps you to stay away from other people's decisions that are made for you so that you will be the ultimate controller of what things you want in your life and how do you plan to reach these things. Being in a powerful place of planning and gearing the ship of your life will take you many steps closer to achieving success.

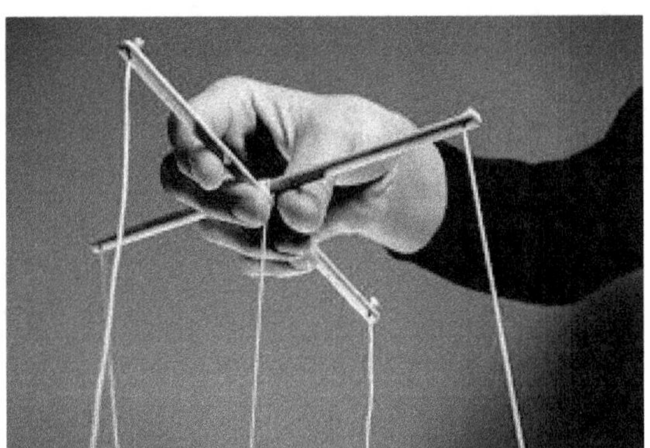

#4 - Planning gives your life a sense of balance

Without planning, it is very easy for all of us to get swayed in the waves of emotions and spend time with unnecessary people or on unnecessary tasks like watching a TV show for hours together. Planning helps you stay focused and guides you in the light of your success. It prevents you from wasting your time and gives a sense of balance to your life. Right planning will give you ample time to manage both work and personal life activities. A perfect balance between work and professional life is only possible when you draw up a plan.

#5 - Planning gives you a sense of direction and purpose in life

It you do not have your life plans in place, you'll be left wandering about and around everything that glitters without ever getting them. Your life will be geared by others and you'll become a mere spectator of what's happening in your own life. Planning is what drives people in the right direction. For example: If you are a Civil Service aspirant, you should have a plan in place in order to become a civil servant. You should enroll yourself to the necessary courses, sign up for a couple of online courses, pay up the examination fees on time and define a study plan that'll help you prepare for the exams.

Similarly, be it any goal of your life - planning is very important to keep you going and it the biggest source of drive and motivation. If you want to attain a healthy body, you should draw up a plan that'll have details about the set of exercises and the diet plans that you'll follow in order to attain your ideal weight. The next step is to stick to this course of plan and take actions in that regard. Without planning, you'll be like a lost child in the jungle having no idea about what to do!

Remember: Without leaps of imagination or dreaming, we lose the excitement of possibilities. Dreaming, after all is a form of planning.

CHAPTER 10 – INNOVATION AND CREATIVITY

Doing the same things over and over again, and expecting to achieve different results is the biggest mistake one can do. However, sadly many ordinary people who struggle to reach success dream of getting different results by doing the same things in the same manner and same environments. If you want to lead an extraordinary life that is filled with happiness and one that fullfils your purpose in your life, it is important that you make a firm decision on changing certain habits, thinking patterns and your overall lifestyle.

One such success habits to develop is Innovation and Creativity. It is said that innovation is the intelligence having fun, but in simple terms - innovation and creativity are closely related and just means to try new things or try things differently. Innovation and creativity can help you find new ways of looking at different situations and come up with solutions that'll solve any obstacle at hand.

Big corporates always encourage their employees to "think out of the box" or to just be very creative and innovative with everything they do. Why do corporates seek and reward employees who are innovative and creative? The simple answer is that there's a newness associated with innovation and creativity, and thus this newness will give raise to solutions which weren't thought out until now and thus helps any company or an organization get better. This isn't true or confined at corporate levels alone.

The same rule can be applied to our lives as well where a little bit of innovation and creativity can change things drastically. Besides, these qualities are like skills which can be developed and honed over time. They help to make your life better, refreshing and more rewarding and fulfilled. Here are some tips which you can try right away to develop the skills of creativity and innovation.

However, bear in mind that these skills cannot be developed by just looking at a few tips. They must be practiced in everyday lives for them to become a part of your life and the results you can achieve from these qualities will be exceptional. Without further ado, let's dive right into the simple yet effective tips you can follow today to enhance your creativity and innovative abilities:

#1 - Commit your mind to developing your creative abilities

The first step is to commit yourself to developing this new skill before you can follow any other tips. Remember that these cannot be developed overnight and require consistent efforts and dedication from your end. All the other tips would go in vain if you cannot get yourself to commit to this goal. Make it a goal like your other goals and give it all the due importance that it deserves. Be persistent and motivate yourself every time you feel bogged down with low motivation. Put certain amount of time aside each day towards developing this skill. It is just like any other new skill that you want to develop and will take considerable amount of time.

Thus, prepare your mind well in advance to be ready to this commitment before you practice the next tips.

#2 - Be naturally curious and allow yourself to explore

One major roadblocks to developing creativity and innovative abilities is a sense of feeling that being curious is a waste of time. Break this myth in your mind and understand that genuine creativity and innovation stems from natural curiosity. When you're stuck with some project, take the time out to understand why you're stuck and let yourself to explore your doubts and queries. Have questions and develop a questioning mind. Start questioning everything about anything that is not setting in pace. In the process of doing so, your mind will automatically open up to the idea of having different sets of perspectives about anything at hand. Different perceptions allows you to think of different possibilities and different ways of looking at situations, boosting your creativity.

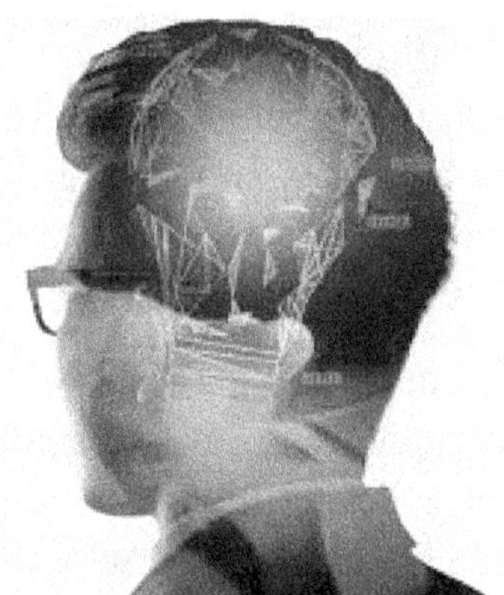

#3 - Be willing to fail and do not fear failure

Fear of failure has killed more dreams than failure ever has! This is extremely true and you'll find so many examples to prove this. No scientific innovation was done in a day, or in the very first go. Everybody has gone through many failures before they've become successful at something. Fearing failure is a negative attitude that cirbs creativity and innovation and stops you from trying and exploring at all. Be willing to fail and understand that failures are great learning opportunities for you to get closer to your success. This attitude helps you become more of a doer who's not afraid of commuting mistakes. Creativity sparks high in such situations where you're not chaining your mind with the fear of failure.

#4 - Brainstorm with your friends and inspire new ideas!

Remember that every problem can be solved in not one, but often in many ways. Talking to various people about similar topics can open up your perspective and give you many different type of thought processes. These will help you to come up with new ideas for different problems. Keep asking yourself - what can I do different this time? Or imagine yourself in the shoes of someone who is already an expert, for example, your senior manager and think - How would my manager tackle this? What would I be thinking if I were my manager? These simple mind shifts might seem silly at the outlook but they go a long way in changing how you think and approach your problems altogether.

#5 - Indulge in habits that boost your creativity

There are certain hobbies or habits that boosts our creativity and innovation muscles and this is different for everyone. Playing guitar might get someone to feel creative, listening to classical music might do the trick for another, playing a favourite sport might be the answer to some others. What is yours? What are your habits or hobbies that you love doing and derive pleasure and happiness from? List them out and set aside certain amount of time every day to indulge yourself in these hobbies. Allow yourself to have fun and just be present. When your mind feels relaxed, you are more prone to coming up with creative and innovative solutions that do not come to surface when you're stressed.

#6 - Expand your knowledge

It goes unsaid that often our creative and innovative abilities are limited because we fear that a solution that we think is new has already been tried and tested, and probably failed. However, on the contrary, many new ideas that we think of may not have been tried. That's the whole point of corporates always trying to push their employees to constantly think out of the box. If you feel limited by this and have a self-doubt that you just don't know enough about a subject that'll enable you to come up with creative solutions, it's best to work on expanding your knowledge about that particular subject. Read as much as you can about the subject you're trying to learn. Indulge yourself in it and master it. Once you've done that, your brain is much more susceptible to conceiving new ideas and to also put them forth across a bunch of people as you now don't have the fear of coming across as a stupid person.

Here's a small inspirational poem that you can mark and read when you feel you're running out

of your creative juices, which might help you get right back on track:

Good ideas will take you places.

Sometimes I just like to think,

And capture my ideas in ink.

When the pen begins to flow,

I leave my thoughts and let them go.

It's when the mind starts to run free,

That we really do begin to see.

Our eyes are somehow opened wide,

And we are given a peek inside.

We see the place where ideas grow,

The one's with passion we must sow.

Big ideas can give us power,

They bloom and grow just like a flower.

Tricky problems simply pop,

As great ideas take you to the top.

Don't keep them locked up in dark spaces,

Good ideas will take you places.

CHAPTER 11 – VALUE FOR TIME AND TIME MANAGEMENT

Time is the greatest equaliser in life. It treats everybody the same and it is a slave to none. Whether you are rich, poor, student, entrepreneur, housewife, you have the same amount of time as everybody else around you. Regardless of your race, age, gender, religion, nationality, social and income status - you've got the same time as the next person to you. Thus, time is not about how much you're left with but it is about what you intend to do with whatever time you have left with.

Time treats everybody exactly the same and this can be your greatest friend or your greatest enemy depending upon your own perspectives about it and how you manage it. Successful people are known to be masters of their time and they know a great deal about effective time management. No human is a robot who can run on a constant autopilot mode without sleep or fun in between work. However, some humans tend to perform better at work, have healthy and strong relationships and have a positive outlook towards their lives, while others are seen whining about their time management problems and how they just cannot get themselves to completing any project at hand.

If you are someone who finds yourself complaining about the shortage of time very frequently, you should take serious and conscious steps in this direction for a better and an effective time management, or the time will get the better of you and your life will pass you by without you even realising about the same. An effective time management is a must have skill for any individual who is driven by ambitious goals. Here are some top tips on effective time management that are simple to follow with results that'll stun you, if you do it persistently and effectively.

#1 - Have a daily routine

Most people have routines in their lives but not many of them have the right routine which works for them. Having a right daily routine that works for you and brings you effective results is very important. Your routine must consist of all the activities that are important to you and ones which take you closer to your dreams and your overall success in your life. Having a routine that only focuses on few key aspects will not give you great results in the end. A daily routine begins right from the exercise workouts you plan for yourself to what you include in your diet, followed by your work schedule and the things you want to do in your spare time everyday. A complete routine cannot be achieved in a single day. You need to make consistent tweaks to your routine to finally find something that works right for you. If you are an entrepreneur, you should definitely set time aside to read news and updates about what's happening in the entrepreneurial world and how it might affect your business. Based on your own dreams and goals, design a routine that's unique to you and works for you. Having a daily routine helps immensely in sticking to your dream goals and without it, you might feel a little too caught up in unimportant or unnecessary things like scrolling through your social media or checking out random YouTube videos which won't add any real value to your life.

#2 - Prioritize your tasks

We all have a list of the many things that we want to do everyday, every week and every month. These tasks will carry different levels of priority and importance based on how soon we want to get them done and how rewarding are the end results. Having too many goals can often get in the way of achieving these very goals. That does not mean you should go about cutting down your goals, but what you can is to prioritize your goals or tasks.

Mark which ones are the most important for you right now and plan your days and weeks accordingly. For example: If scaling up your business is your primary goal for the month, include and prioritize more tasks that will take to close to realizing this goal, like reading business updates, hiring the right people to expand your team, getting your business resources in place and so on. On the other hand, if attaining a target weight goal is your primary goal, prioritize and follow through all those tasks that are linked to fitness, like waking up at a certain time every morning and following a strict workout routine, eating right, strength training and so on. Without prioritizing your tasks, the chances are that you'll get too caught up in doing things that will not serve your goal of reaching success.

#3 - Avoid wastage of time and be mindful of where you're investing your time

Saying NO to things you don't want to indulge in is one of the most important qualities that is practiced by successful people. They take no guilt in turning down their friends when they have other more important tasks at hand to attend to. You should avoid wasting time on parties or other social gatherings that will take up too much of your time and energies, without making you very happy. All work and no play makes Jack a dull boy, is true, and you should be having fun as you work your way up towards fulfilling your goals but remember to realize when you're crossing the lines and making fun a primary priority in your life. Say NO to things which do not help you in your pursuit of happiness and success. Additionally, be very mindful of where you're investing your time. What you do throughout your day, matters and contributes to what you do throughout your week, a month and an year too!

#4 - Set your own deadlines

It is true that most people love to procrastinate on things that do not provide them instant and immediate gratification. For this reason, setting up your own deadlines is very important. Whether it is your personal goal of achieving a certain target weight goal, visiting a couple of tourist places, increasing your business revenue, scaling up your business, getting that hike or promotion at your job, setting up your side hustle, creating some passive income for yourself, or any other goal that you're pursuing right now, without attaching a date or a deadline to it, chances are you won't make any real progress. Write down what you want to achieve and write down the timeline before which you intend to accomplish this goal. You want to lose a certain amount of weight, don't stop at that. Define by what time you want to reach that goal. This method will keep you measured and focused, taking you closer to accomplishing your dreams.

Remember these words by Anthony Robbins that stress on the importance of effective time management:

Once you have mastered time, you will understand how true it is that most people overestimate what they can accomplish in a year – and underestimate what they can achieve in a decade!

CHAPTER 12 – STRESS AND CRISES MANAGEMENT

All kind of changes, whether big or small, indices some levels of stress in humans. Regardless of your age, gender, occupation, caste or creed - stress is a problem all of us face in our lives. The degree of stress varies from person to person but it is something we cannot totally escape from. Stress is one of most common problems for everyone and you're not alone if you feel very stressed out at times of anxiety. However, learning how to manage stress is a skill not many of us learn in the school of life. What we do with all the built up stress and how we choose to cope with it defines the overall quality of our life.

If you look at the life of highly effective and successful people, you'll notice that these people often have many things to think about and often can find themselves in highly stressful situations as compared to ordinary people. Great entrepreneurs of the world like Jeff Bezos, Tim Cook, Mark Zuckerberg have giant companies to run and great CEOs like Sundar Pichai have a mammoth of tasks and responsibilities to fulfill and yet you never see them complain about stress being a big problem. What does this mean? Does it indicate an absence of stress in their lives? Certainly not.

These are some of the most powerful and influential people on the planet and they cannot be stress-free. So, what really sets them apart? The trick lies in effective management of stress. We all have stress. Even a school going kid will have certain percentage of stress attached, nobody can escape it. However, how we choose to deal with stress defines who we become.

Managing your stress effectively can come a long way not only in ensuring that you feel happy and are productive, but also in determining how soon you'll reach your success and the overall quality of your life. Life only gets more stressful by the day, as you grow up and assume more roles and responsibilities. Learning to cope with stress acts as a shield that will save you a lot of pain and take you closer to achieving your dreams.

Besides, we can also often find ourselves in stressful situations that go well beyond the routine work stress, which might create havoc in our lives, making our days harder and harder. Demise of a loved one, loss of a job, loss of a position, a hurtful breakup, a painful incident that caused trauma, witnessing something extremely shocking, betrayal from a loved one, loss of an opportunity that you've waited for too long etc can lead to extremely stressful times where simple everyday tasks might seem like a lot to do! Just getting through the day too might seem like a huge task and such times lead to crises in your life.

If you do not manage your crises effectively, it can very adversely and negatively impact your life, pushing to an even darker place from which you cannot get out of. An effective stress management helps you cope with your routine stress, and an effective crises management helps you pull your life together when it's falling apart and when you feel very hopeless about your situation. Remember that every person goes through dark and painful times! How you bounce back from it determines the quality of your life. Here are a few very healthy ways of coping with stress and how to effectively manage crises.

#1 - Prioritize and focus on what is very important to you

During a time of crises, it is very important that you be kind to yourself and focus on things that are the most important ones for you. Prioritize tasks which you should get done and check off all the most important tasks from the list before you move on to mundane routine tasks for the rest of the day. For example: Having a certain number of work meetings every week might be very necessary to you, so ensure that your top focus is always on this and cut off other tasks which have less priority, like hiring a new employee.

#2 - Calm yourself down at times of stress and think of new perspectives of looking at your situation

This might sound very hard but its importance cannot be stressed more as it is extremely necessary especially in the time of a dire crises. Calming yourself down is extremely important for you to be able to feel light and think about other things which matter to you. A painful or a shocking incident that has happened lies in the past, and it's best you make your peace with the past so that you can get up and going about your life. Think of fresh perspectives of looking at your situation.

For example: Let's say you got cheated on by your partner in business and you'll have to now build a new business, all from the scratch. Instead of stopping at just crying about it or feeling self-pity and all the sadness, which are natural primary responses, move on and try to think of other perspectives of looking at your situation. Think about the silver linings that this dark cloud in your life had. Think about the things it taught you. Think about how you're now more capable and can do business in a much better fashion, now that you've parted your ways with a cheatful partner who taught you the lessons you needed to learn, and so on and so forth. This change in perception is a great way of coping and it'll help you rise beyond the crises, and come out stronger than before.

#3 - Surround yourself with kind, supportive and caring people who love you

At a time of crises, it is so important to be surrounded by the right people. Having people throw tantrums at you first thing in the morning when you're already dealing with a lot of stress in your mind is the last thing you want. Surround yourself with kind people who understand that you've been through something very stressful and who'll be there for you to listen you out and give you some relief.

These people could be your family or friends, but ensure that you have your support circle strong during a stressful situation. Do not feel guilty about seeking out for help. Remember that the people who really love you and care for you will want to stay by your side as you battle your demons. Crises in life can make or break you for your entire life, and you have every right to seek help from your loved ones. Be vocal about the issues you're facing and talk to your near and dear ones from time to time. Many people resort to self-isolation during a time of crises or just a stressful period but doing that is only going to do you more harm than good. So, be around people and talk with them, and let them help you with your crises management.

#4 - Process your feelings

Feeling a vast surge of emotions during stressful times is very common for all of us and processing these feelings effectively is very important to get past your trauma. Ignoring how you're feeling about something and trying to get lost in an indulgence or an addiction might seem like an immediate escape, but these paths will only take you downhill. Instead, approach and embrace a more healthy approach of processing your feelings. Process them through and write them down in a journal.

Whether it is writing down in a journal, taking to a friend or just consulting a good therapist, do whatever it takes for you to be able to process your feelings better. Do this diligently and you'll feel more relieved and relaxed at the end of doing it. Bottling up your emotions inside isn't going to do any good for your emotional and mental well-being.

#5 - Be kind and patient with yourself

It is very common for many people to take a more self-destructive approach of beating oneself down during a time of crises. For example: A lot of people who lose their spouses start blaming themselves for the demise of their partner and start punishing themselves in guilt and remorse. These attitudes give raise to behaviours of being rude with oneself or having extremely unrealistic or unreasonable expectations from oneself.

Such techniques will add to the existing stress and will only keep pushing you over the brink. Be kind to yourself during crises. Let yourself feel the pain and don't have high expectations from yourself until you dig yourself out of it. Doing greatly at your job or your business might be the last thing on your list when you've just been through a traumatic experience in your life. Give yourself the time you need to recover from it and embrace yourself with all the kindness that you have until you recover yourself from the crises or the impending trauma.

CHAPTER 13 – THE RIGHT BELIEF SYSTEMS

Great people are born, not made. Are they born the moment they come to the world as babies? No. They are born the moment they recognize and realize the power of their inner beliefs! Inner beliefs define the way you look at the world. Each one of us are looking at the world with our own pair of lens - ***our belief systems.*** That is the reason each one of us have a different perception of the same world. To some people, world is a boring place with all the gloomy and dull things. While to some others, world is a happy place with all the happy and cheerful things. Whatever you believe as the truth of the world, is the truths of the world for you. Whatever you believe people are, they are, for you. If you believe a person is great, your mind will find all the reasons that support this belief. On the other hand, if you believe a person is a total creep, the same mind will find all the reasons that says he is a creep!

Let us take an example of falling in love. When you fall in love with a person and see going through the first stages of love, you totally love all the traits and all the qualities of the person you have fallen in love with. Does that mean this person you are in love with has no qualities that you don't like? Absolutely not! Every person has their own set of good and not-so-good qualities. So, why is it that you are so blinded to the traits of the person who is your new found love?

The reason is that you strongly believe that this person is the best match for you! You strongly believe that you like everything about this person. And it is this strong belief that makes you overlook the traits which you don't like. They are there. All kinds of traits are always there. But in the initial stages of your relationship, you totally overlook them. This is the reason that many people complain about the not desirable qualities in their partners after some time has been passed in the relationship. Until that phase, everything about the partner and the relationship is absolutely beautiful and amazing!

Your inner beliefs about people and world thus, plays a huge, *huge* role in defining your world altogether! If you believe the world is full of people who want to deceive you, you are most likely to spot people who will try to deceive you. **What you focus is what you will find.**

If you are sitting in a room with white walls and filled with objects of different colours, you will not notice any one particular colour in the lot until you consciously look for it. If you look for red colour, you will find things that are red in colour. If you look for things that are yellow, you will find things that are yellow! What you seek is what you will see! So, what is it that you are seeking? Do you seek to live an incredible life? How strong is your belief that you will find it? Whether you will find it or not, is hugely based on how strong your belief really is!

#1 - Your inner beliefs will define outcome of everything that you do

Your inner beliefs are the ones that fuel your actions. If you believe that you can break an egg open using your fingers, you will act on it accordingly and not search for a spoon or a fork to break the egg open. If you believe that you can top at an exam, your actions will also be like a person who can top the exam! Your actions are always in tandem to your beliefs. If your inner belief tells you that you can build a great business only if you invest hugely, you will start finding ways to raise your investments. On the flip side, if your inner belief tells you that you can build a great business even with no or less investments, you will find ways of building a business with no or low investments! Your actions follow your inner beliefs. And your outcomes will follow the actions you've chosen to take.

If you believe you can be incredible, *you can be.* If you believe you can be ten times better and ten times more successful than you are now, *you can be!*

#2 - Your inner beliefs can help you do whatever you want to, and help you be whatever you want to be

There is no superhero on this planet who does not believe he is one! All the superheroes you've ever heard of in your life have the strongest inner beliefs that drive them to take actions which they do! Yes, the Iron Man, the Spider Man, the Batman, the Incredible

Hulk, the Wonder Woman - everybody have strong inner beliefs that they are the heroes the world needs.

If you want to be a highly influential person, and have a strong belief that you really can influence people greatly, greater probabilities are that you will be a great influencer down the line. All achievements humankind has seen in the whole of history started from a belief. Taking actions towards themselves strong inner beliefs is the second step. Beliefs are the most important and primary to actions. And if you wish to change anything in your life, it should start from changing your inner beliefs about it.

Let us assume you have an unsuccessful business set up, before calling up for an expert appointment to see where your business is doing wrong, ask yourself about the beliefs you have about your business. Do you believe that you are the right person to run the show of your business? Do you believe that you have all the resources you think you need to make your business set up a successful venture? Do you believe that all the employees and partners of your business are giving their best to the business? Do you believe, this business is something you really, *really* want to do?

Answering these questions honestly will require you to really get into self retrospection. Most people who do not run a business successfully, are the ones who lack the strong inner belief that this business will be successful. Similarly, most people who do not explore many challenging adventures like hiking, mountaineering, sky diving etc are the ones who lack the strong inner belief that they can rock at these adventures. So, all the trainings they may take, all the learnings they got from all the experts at the field will go in vain if there is no shift in their inner mindsets. You can never be the greatest dancer in the world if you think you cannot be one, if your inner belief dies not suggest that you are the greatest dancer, inspite of all the best trainings you get from all around the world!

Best of the talents go down the drain because of lack of belief! Many people struggling with making a fortune of money strongly believe that the rich get richer and the poor remain poor, this strong inner belief keeps them from exploring all the possibilities of opportunities of growing rich because they are blinded by this belief! So, although they have the drive to be rich, and read many books on how to grow rich, unless they internally believe that they can be rich, they won't move one step ahead from wherever they are! In a nutshell, if you want to be great at something, if you want to be great at anything, you should first believe that you can be great at it in the first place, and only then all the actions that you are taking will be meaningful and will add value to whatever you are doing! If you want to be the greatest dog trainer in the world, believe that you can be one!

#3 - Your inner beliefs will make you strong from the inside

A person with strong inner beliefs will not feel demotivated by the small failures in the beginning. A person who wants to be a great swimmer but does not believe he or she can be a great swimmer, will feel disheartened at the very moment they lose or fail. Strong inner beliefs make people resilient and persistent at their efforts and actions, because it not sole actions they lay their trust in, but the strong belief systems they lay their trust in!

Your inner beliefs will make you shielded from any external influences and failures, you will keep going at it, again and again, even if you are falling and you will finally reach the place you want to reach! You will finally be what you want to be!

#4 - Your inner beliefs will define your realities

If you believe you are not good enough at something, you will listen to every person who tells you that you aren't good enough and disregard the comments of every person who tells you that you are good. If you believe you will be the greatest chef in the world, you will do everything that takes for you to be one, and you will be the greatest chef.

As rightly put by Mahatma Gandhi - *Man often becomes what he believes himself to be. If I keep on saying to myself that I cannot do a certain thing, it is possible that I may end by really becoming incapable of doing it. On the contrary, if I shall have the belief that I can do it, I shall surely acquire the capacity to do it, even if I may not have it at the beginning.*

So, what do you believe about yourself? What are your strongest inner beliefs? Do they tell you that you can be wonderful? Do they tell you that you can discover your fullest potential? Do they tell you, *that you can be incredible?*

Once you have realized the power of inner beliefs and the big role they play in shaping your lives, bringing out the incredible you from you is an easy peasy task. For when you have realized how your inner beliefs can change your life, both for good, or for bad, depending upon the quality of your inner thoughts, you can change all those beliefs that will cripple the incredible person inside you and build up more and more on all those beliefs that will help the same hidden incredible version of you to come to light! ***And, to come to life.***

As rightly said, it is the crazy people who say they will change the world that actually will change the world! The power of belief is the beginning of every worthy journey ever taken in the history of mankind! The belief to do great things is what field you to actually do all those great things!

CHAPTER 14 – GET OUT OF THE BLAME GAME

You definitely do not want the slow poison of playing blame games come in the way of your growth or the overall happiness of your life. Wherever you are now, you can grow into a person even better than who you are now. You can climb much greater heights than what you already have. Successful people are the ones that take responsibility for their mistakes and they don't get trapped in the constant blame game. Snapping out of a blame game is so important for you to achieve success in any part of your life. Here are a few things you can do today to stop the blame game.

#1 - Take ownership of your failures

If you fail at something, before blaming anything or anyone, take ownership of it. Stop thinking in the lines which would suggest that it is everyone else, *but you* who is responsible for your failure. Start thinking in the lines where you hold yourself responsible for your failures. If you have failed, *you* have failed. That is all there is. That is *all* the truth is.

You need to look at what made you fail, maybe you weren't good enough, maybe you needed more preparation, maybe your estimates went wrong, maybe the data you collected was insufficient, or maybe a hundred other things. Figure out the reason for your failure rather than pointing out other people and situations that made you fail at it.

Let us take an example of competitive exams. When you fail in competitive examinations, how foolish will it be for you to blame the examination question paper setting committe because they set a paper so hard that you couldn't crack it? Does it make sense? Won't you laugh at someone if they told you they failed because of the brainless bunch of people sitting in the examination committee who set a paper that is harder than a nut? Wouldn't you just say "Hey, stop blaming the tough question paper. You were probably not prepared enough for it"?

Most of us are great at pointing out when someone else is playing the blame game but are so poor in pointing out when we ourselves are *rocking* at this needless game! Own your failures and only then, will you be able to make a change. If you don't, you will end up giving up because you genuinely believe that it is not *you*, but other things and people that are real culprits, so there's really nothing much *you* can do about it!

#2 - Take ownership of your successes too!

Just like it is important to own up to your failures, it is important that you own up to your successes too! If you have cracked a tough examination, it is because of your genuine efforts and not because the question paper was so *easy!* If you have got that promotion you were longing for since a long time, it is because you worked hard for it, not because you were randomly chosen by your management. If you climb the Mount Everest, it is because of your mountaineering skills, not because the mountain spirit helped you!

Learn to pat your own back when you feel you're done a great job, it is also as important as learning to own up your failures. Owning your success gives you the needed strength to feel responsible towards the failures you have had.

#3 - Learn a lesson from a mishappening - Shift your focus towards the learnings

So you got badly drenched in the rain and you won't be able to show up at that important office meeting. That is a mishappening. Instead of blaming the rain Gods (who by the way, are really not listening or have their own reasons to pour down waters), learn from it and take precautions the next time you step out. With every *'unlucky'* thing or misfortune that happens with you, learn something.

If you have lost great deal of money in the business, shift your focus towards knowing what went wrong and how you should be fixing it. You can blame your partners or clients all day long, but is that going to make any difference in your business? No. Then, why waste so much time towards blaming?

#4 - Recognize the pattern when you start blaming other people or things

More often than not, there are some sentences that you use a lot when you enter the blaming mode. You will feel angry, frustrated and stressed about the little things around you when you enter this dangerous blame game mode. And when you have, your flow of thoughts clearly flows in your language. You maybe using sentences like - *Oh, but people at office never help me! Oh, but my mother loves my brother more than me. Oh, right, just like always, bad luck always runs behind me. Oh, I'm the only one that never gets a promotion at office because my boss just hates me. Oh, the tailor loves to mess up only with my clothes. Oh, the horrendous traffic will never let me reach on time.*

These are normal ways a master player at the game of blaming gets into the blaming mode. I'm sure you can point out how *you* do it. Doing this is important because that makes you **aware**. It makes the *'Oh, I'm entering the blaming mode and I should stop it right now'* switch go green and you'll know you've started to blame others and must stop. Be very aware of this light going green, and immediately snap out of it. Relax and think how you, could perhaps be the reason and not others.

#5 - Be more empathetic and understanding of others, and of yourself

So what if the office boy at your office added double the sugar you usually take today? Instead of immediately snapping at him, take calm and be empathetic towards him. Mistakes happen by everyone and you should be more understanding of these mistakes. *He's probably having a stressful day today. He probably confused your cup of coffee with someone else's who prefers more sugar. He's probably got 60 cups of coffee to make everyday, and he goofed up today with the sugar added in your cup.*

Try to be more empathetic. You don't have to drink that coffee, you can probably ask him to replace it and he'll do it. So, why create a big fuss about it and spoil your moods, and his day? When somebody has messed up something for you, try to be an empath. Empathize with them and ask them for corrections because, to err is human.

Similarly, also understand your own emotions and setbacks before going on a self-blaming rant. You probably went over dressed for an office party, because you really had no idea that rest of them would keep their dressing so simple, or maybe because you were mocked at in the last office meeting for being under dressed. Tell yourself that *it is okay, it is fine*, you are only a human. Don't punish yourself or blame yourself. Learn from it and make a mental note of asking a couple of colleagues at work about how they'll be dressing, if that's something that's very important to you. **Bottom line: When mistakes happen, pick up a lesson and apply it henceforth. There is no point in blame ranting, regardless of whether it is directed at others or yourself.**

#6 - Learn to accept the genuine compliments that come your way. You deserve it!

Some people are overly modest and can never take genuine compliments. This could be because they don't believe they deserve it or maybe because they believe it is good manners to act all modest when someone compliments. Both of these do not serve any purpose.

The ones that believe they don't deserve the genuine compliments are the ones who self-sabotage. Self-sabotage is a sub conscious thing where people feel inferior to others, even when other people have not intended it. If you meet a person who you think is smarter than you, and you try to disconnect with that person because you think that this smart person is too good and you don't deserve to hang out with people who are so smart, then you're most likely self-sabotaging. And when you are doing that, you can never take a genuine compliment at the face of it.

If somebody thinks you deserve a compliment, it means they *really* think you're good at it. That is *all* there is. Take your compliments well and in the way compliments are intended - *a gesture to tell you that you've been amazing!* Feel good that you have been amazing! Do not immediately just thank someone else or shift the credit of your success and achievements onto others! As I said, own your successes and own the compliments that come along your way!!

When you learn to accept compliments the way it is, you will also learn to accept the blames of your failures on you. You cannot get better at one by ignoring the other. They go hand in hand. **In a nutshell, remember that, good results or bad results, they are both YOURS to own! Own them both!**

#7 - Start responding rather than reacting!

Like in my example of brand new shoes turning brown because of that muddy road, what good is going to happen if you get so upset about it and go on a monologue blaming the government and all the political parties? Shouldn't you be thinking about what you could do about it now? You could probably go back to your home, change the shoes if you've got time, or try cleaning them as much as possible, or just letting it be and tell what happened if someone asks you the mystery behind your brown shoes. You can do anything.. when you respond to what happened rather than resort to reacting to whatever happened. Even if you start reacting for some time, snap out of it within some time and see what can be done **NOW**. Respond to your situations. Learn to let go of reacting.

#8 - Take full responsibility of your life - Believe that it is YOU and only you, who can change things in your life, for good or bad

Be in charge of your life. If the maid has left the floor very slippery and wet, you should probably ask her to make sure it's all dried up, switch on the fan or mop the wet floors with a dry cloth or anything she thinks she should do to keep the floors dry. If she still persists the same habit of leaving behind the floors slippery and you can't take it anymore, you should probably consider changing your maid. Whatever the situation is, learn to be in charge of your life. Believe genuinely that it is YOU who can change your life and you alone.

If you are in a relationship that makes you unhappy, you can either talk about your issues with your partner and see if you can sort it out, or put an end to your relationship. It is very difficult and an unhappy journey to just stay, blame, go through pain and suffering. You either do something about it, and if it doesn't work, you should considering parting ways. You either choose to fix things and stay happy or choose to walk out because it cannot be fixed and stay happy. There is no staying in between.

CHAPTER 15 – BUILD GREAT PERSONAL RELATIONSHIPS

Relationships are a massive part of our lives. Personal relationships with near and dear ones often impact our moods and also contributes to our overall well-being. Humans are social animals. We cannot do without our best relationships with our dear friends and most loved family members. Maintaining positive, healthy and happy relationships isn't always the easiest thing to do and of course, there will be testing times when we do not feel like nurturing our personal relationships.

However, taking good amount of interest and investing good amount of time into our relationships can come a long way in ensuring that we live happy and successful lives. Happiness comes from sharing good times with our loved ones! And yet, so many people struggle with building and maintaining healthy and happy interpersonal relationships. The value of maintaining personal relationships often gets very overlooked as people get busy chasing their professional dreams and building a career for themselves.

However, at the end of the day, it is our friends and families who will be there with us during the hard times and who make our journey of life worthwhile. If you've been struggling with maintaining strong and happy Relationships in your personal life, here are some simple tips you can follow today that'll make your journey a happier one and fill your life with happiness. This will surely give you a great internal boost which'll push you towards your goals. Besides, who doesn't want to love and be loved? All of us do!

So here are some really small yet very effective efforts you can start putting in right from today to build and nurture your relationships. At the end the day, remember that relationships are like flowers. You need to carefully nurture them and pour in your time and efforts with love to make them work. You can also use these tips to enhance or further strengthen your existing Relationships. A great family bonding and a great friendship circle will both go a long run to ensure that you get the very best from your life. Read on and start your journey to building happy and strong personal relationships that last and hold you tight together!

#1 - Keep in touch with your near and dear ones

This may sound like an absolute no-brainer but it's appalling to notice that most of us fail to actively keep in touch with our near and dear ones. Forgetting to return calls from friends and family, forgetting their important dates like birthdays, skipping meeting with them and saying no to them when they want to hang out together have all become too common these days. Now, one can find a hundred excuses or reasons for not catching up and not keeping in touch. However, if you really hold someone dear, it is only fair that you keep in active touch with them from time to time.

Check up on them and ask them how they're doing. Sometimes, a simple message that asks about someone's day can put a smile on people's face. Actively engage in keeping up with your personal relationship and do not give lane excuses to cancel meeting with your loved ones. Regardless of how advanced our technology is and how well inter connected we all are through our social media, nothing beats a face to face communication. Focus on meeting with your loved ones if you wish to keep them near and close to your heart.

#2 - Focus on creating quality time together with your friends and families

Everyone has their own set of friends, who they meet during different times of the week. You might have a bunch of office friends with whom you catch up everyday with. And then, there would be friends from your college or school who you might meet once in a month. Whatever the frequency of your meetings, ensure to create some quality time together with them.

Remember that quality time isn't the same as spending a few hours in a month with someone. It is about truly involving in their lives and understanding what is going on in their life, to listen out to what they're saying and to respond to them effectively from time to time. Spend good quality time with your friends and use this time to feel refreshed and rejunevated in your life. Talk and discuss about your goals, how you're doing, where you wish to be a few months down the line and so on.

These strong and quality inter personal communications with your friends will not only strengthen your bond with them, but will also come a long way in building a certain amount of social security in your life where you are prone to feeling more emotionally secure and safe as you always have someone to count on!

Similar rule applies to your relationship with your family members as well. Spend good family time with your spouse and children. Understand them and learn more about them. Don't stop at knowing their likes and dislikes. Go beyond that and understand what makes them very happy, what makes them sad or angry, what fulfills them, what are their goals in life, how are they doing mentally or emotionally and much much more. Try to put in your time and efforts to truly know and understand your family members.

#3 - Be a good listener and truly listen your dear ones out

While you're talking with your loved ones, the last thing you should be doing is to make them feel like you're not paying attention to them. Being a bad listener can really dampen the quality of your relationship with anyone. Be a good listener and pay full attention to what someone is trying to tell you. Understand their perspectives and respect their thinking, even if you don't fully agree with it.

The way you listen to someone determines whether or not this person would love to being their problems back to you or even talk to you again. The best example for this can be noticed in little children. Children are generally talkative and they like to share every detail of what happened during their day with their parents. However, if parents continually ignore their kids while they're talking and pay attention to something else, children will slowly start drifting apart from their parents and stop talking about their day.

This is true for other relationships too. Whether it is a romantic relationship that you want to build on or a friendship that you want to develop or strengthen, not listening enough is one of the biggest hurdles that'll stand between you and your dear one. Practice active listening as a part of your daily life and you'll notice that people will be draw to you as every one of us crave for caring listening ears!

#4 - Help your loved ones to make their lives better

Try to help your loved ones with any issues that they may be facing, even when they're not actively seeking for your help. Take a deep look into their lives and you'll get an understanding of what areas of life your loved ones might be having issues with. Discuss with them about these issues and lend them in a helping hand. If it is your spouse or a close friend, sometimes just an understanding and a listening ear might be very helpful for them. Be there for your loved ones when they need you.

And sometimes, it can get tricky for people to seek out someone's help especially when our lives get very busy. During such times, if you can take up the initiative of asking and helping out your loved ones will instantly make them very happy. They might not really ask for a huge favour from you but just done motivating and supportive words perhaps will do the trick!

#5 - Don't take your relationships for granted

Taking your relationships for granted is perhaps the most damaging thing you can do in your relationship. Yet, most of us are pros at doing this. We can get too caught up in our own lives and get too comfortable with our personal relationships, slowing we start taking these relationships for granted and later wonder - what happened to my best friend? Why is my spouse not talking with me as much? What happened to that co-worker who always came to me with her problems? It might be too late by then. Don't take them for granted. Yes, these relationships might be working very well for now and moving on very perfectly but that doesn't mean that you should stop putting in your efforts to make them better. Constantly try to make your relationships better!

#6 - Let your loved ones know that you love them!

This one goes unsaid but it's so important to stress on this because most people fail to do this. We get too caught up and forget the importance of letting our dear ones know that we love them! Doing small little things to make them happy or getting something they really love are just some ways of showing them you truly love them. It is important that you tell your loved ones how much you love them. Take time out of your schedule to plan something really special for your spouse every week, or at the least, every month. Such little efforts will truly make their worlds and they'll be so thrilled to have you in their lives! Showing your gratitude towards them goes a long way in building and strengthening your bond with them!

#7 - Be a part of their lives and make them a part of yours!

One great way of strengthening your bond with a loved one is to be a part of their lives actively. This means to understand what is going on in their lives, what are they upto during their free time, what dreams or goals they are chasing, what makes them most happy, what puts them on a cloud nine, who are their most valued relationships, what plans do they have for their vacation and so on. Being involved with someone's life requires you to really listen out to them while they're talking and pay close attention to details that most matter to them. These things might seem very little, but these little things are the ones that truly build a great bonding.

Remembering what is going on in someone's life and checking up on them from time to time is a great way to make your way into someone's heart! Similarly, make them a part of your life too. Tell them what are the things which are most important to you. Let them know about the goals that you are chasing and about the dream experiences that you wish to live! Make a bucket list of traveling or any other sort of adventure together and try to do it together. Celebrate their little victories and throw them a party when you've accomplished something too! Such little things can really change and strengthen your relationships in way you cannot imagine!

CHAPTER 16 – CHASE YOUR DREAMS

Every person has big dreams! Some go at it and some do not. If you haven't gone at your dreams and you are reading this now, I'm so happy to tell you all the good reasons why you should be chasing your dreams. And if these reasons do not convince you, and you believe you cannot make your dreams come true, you must change your inner beliefs! I have talked about the impact and power of your inner beliefs in the later part of this book. But if it's not lack of belief in your dream, but a lack of motivation or purpose, I really think the following reasons will convince you to chase your dreams!

#1 - Dreams keep you going and ALIVE

Without dreams, you have nothing better than '*what you already have*' to look forward to. Dreams add life to your hopes and hopes fuel life. They keep you alive and the moment you start dreaming big things, you'll cease to '*just exist*' and *start to live!* There will be so much life around everything and about everything. Small things which must have looked so boring or even, unnoticeable will start to look beautiful.

When you have something better to look forward to, you wake up with bright eyes and trust me, you will glow differently. When you dream, you'll feel ALIVE! And that's how you'll be different from others who're just going about their mundane lives. You become different because your dreams have ignited the life spark inside you and you're now chasing your dreams. *Top speed!*

#2 - Dreams wake up the employees in your brains and keep you mentally so active that you cannot imagine!

People with dreams have their little employees in their minds that are going all jumping, saying "*Wow. I have a beautiful day ahead of me and I am running towards my dreams, getting closer to realizing it by each passing day!*". On the other hand, people with no dreams have lazy little employees in their minds making their mundane lives all the more boring. I would say that 85% of their employees are just plain dead or sleeping because, they have NOTHING to do! While the remaining 15% is awake just to keep them alive and wake them up to their typical '*same mundane day everyday*'.

For them, every day is the same. Every new day won't be different than the days in the past and they start working like a programmed robot. Do you want to function and lead your life like a programmed robot? Is yes, then do not dream. If not, then, you *must* DARE to dream!

#3 - Dreams rule your thoughts. And what you think, you become

Your thoughts are influenced by your dreams. If you dream of riding a Ferrari on highways, your mind will be full of thoughts where you're driving a Ferrari and not a Maruthi 800. If you dream of being the greatest chef, your thoughts will be likewise too. You won't end up becoming a temple priest if you're dreaming of being a business millionaire. Similarly, you'll never become an incredible person if you don't dream to become one. And it is these dreams that rule over your thoughts.

When you go to car showroom and start checking out different cars, you must have observed how salespersons there would convince you into going on a test drive. Even if you're not planning to buy the car, they'll convince you for a test drive saying, '*Just take a test drive sir. Just take a small ride madam*' and almost always, we all try it.

Why do you think it's such a huge selling proposition? It is because these guys know that once they get you behind the steering wheel, the deal is almost done and sealed! They very reason why they insist on a test drive so much is that they want you to feel and experience how it is like to drive that car. They're making you dream about it and the physical hands on experience will make you all the more willing to buy it. Because, your dream of buying a car when you entered into the showroom has now become more concrete. And in most cases, people end up buying. That's how car sales are done. **Bottom-line: Dreams become thoughts. Thoughts are envisioned. And they turn into realities!**

Any person who has accomplished wild results in history had first dreamt about it. Dreams enable you to envision what you want. And the next easy job for your brain is to just focus on things that'll help you assemble all you want to convert what you envision as your dream into your realities. For any reality to happen, it must be dreamt of first. Every single person who has went on to accomplish crazy things can attest this truth. Dreams precede the realities, every single time. Your realities talk a great deal about your dreams! And your dreams will determine your realities.

#4 - Your focus drifts towards your dreams

When you have dreams, your mind focuses towards achieving those dreams. And, what you *focus on,* you get *more of.* Here's an interesting story about focus. It's my favorite story and I talk about it everytime I'm talking about focus in my seminar.

Two friends in London always dreamt of going to luxurious lavish parties. They planned to save money for some time and somehow manage to make it to one of the most happening parties in London. They were very focused towards it and they finally managed to save up enough to make it to the party. **The** big party of their lives. They got all nicely dressed up and went to the party. Both of them were super excited about it.

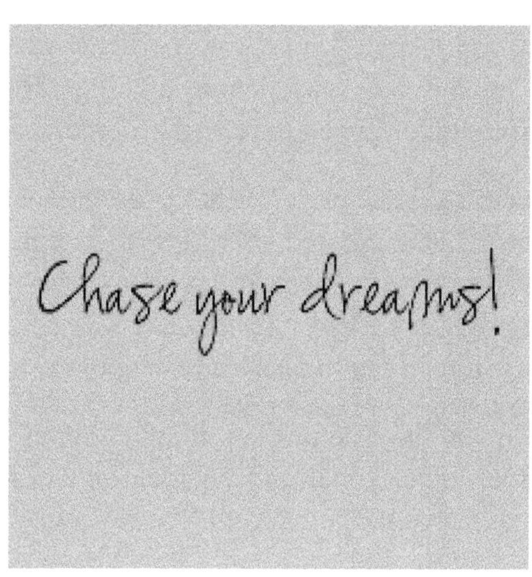

After the party was over, they came back and when they spoke of how the party turned out to be with their other common friends, they had completely different stories to tell altogether! For a moment, their friends doubted if both of them went to the same party.

While one them said the party was so full of fun that it was one of the finest nights of his life, the other one had to tell that he was rather totally disappointed with the party and it was a horrible experience for him. While one said, he'd die to go to such parties again, the other said he'd never even think of going to such parties ever again in his life. When the shocked friends asked them about what each one of them did, they learnt about why the same party appeared to be so different for both of them.

The first friend enjoyed himself by dancing, laughing, meeting new people, making new friends and got back believing it was a wonderful experience. Whereas, the second friend caught hold of a gloomy couple in one of the shady corners of the club as soon as he entered and he watched them endlessly argue and bicker. As he moved his eyes around, he noticed more such couples and groups having heated arguments. That's why he believed that the party was awful as all he saw was people arguing. The two friends focused on different things and thus, had different experiences!

What is the moral of the story? Whatever you focus on, grows. Had the second friend ignored this gloomy couple and brushed them aside because he was there to have fun and not watch stupid arguments, he might have had fun! It could have been the best day of his life. But it turned out to be awful and gloomy.

Similarly, when you have no dreams, there's nothing great for your mind to focus on. And you'll end up focusing on non-sense like *what other people are doing, what are the arguments happening in your neighbor's house* and what not! Your thoughts are not to be blamed here because, it is you, who has failed to give your thoughts something concrete, something big to focus upon!!

Dream big and you'll be stunned to see how you'll stop giving a piece of your mind to those *petty talks happening in the neighborhood or to the heated debates people are having in your office.* Dreams make your focus shift towards it. And thus, your dream grows, bigger and better by the day and it'll soon manifest into your reality.

#5 - Your achievements will start stacking up!

If you don't dream big, you'll never accomplish the smaller goals you've set to conquer your dream. That's the biggest problem with non-dreamers. They have no big dreams at all, so they end up being the *same* person, every passing year. Have you noticed how some people don't change at all even after years of not seeing them? I'm not talking about their fitness. I'm talking about the careers, the accomplishments they've done, the new limits they've reached, the horizons they've conquered, the new places they've been to... And so on!

It shocks me to see people not change a bit and wish 'Happy new year' on the new year's eve without being a little new than what they were last year. It shocks me. It disturbs me even, at times. Non dreamers do not have any accomplishments stacking up in their life accounts.

That's not at all the case with the dreamers. They'll have lots of new things to share every new year and they would have done different things. I love the sparkle in the eyes of people when they're talking to me about what new they've done last year, what dreams they've accomplished and what new dreams they now have to chase. That's the thing with dreamers. They always dream and they have a whole new list of dreams the moment they've achieved previous dreams. Dreams just do not exhaust for dreamers.

But for non-dreamers, life appears to be very boring always. More often than not, dreamers continue to be dreamers and non-dreamers continue to be non-dreamers. And for non-dreamers, life can get so mundane that they'll not even realize what they're missing out on! If you're not a person with big dreams, break the patterns NOW. Take action now, wake up the dreamer who's sleeping inside you, and start dreaming. Start dreaming already! And you'll be amazed to see your achievements and happy experiences stacking up!! But first, get in action and stack up your dreams!

CHAPTER 18 - TAKE FULL OWNERSHIP OF YOUR LIFE!

It is very easy to complain about all the wrong things going on in our life. However, it takes courage to admit that we are ones who are fully responsible for our mistakes and it is us who must be taking our lives into our control and steer it accordingly. Blaming others is very easy but taking full ownership of one's life is hard. And that is the quality of successful people which separates them from unsuccessful people. Playing the blame game truly can cause too much unhappiness in your life. Here are a few convincing reasons on why should stop the blame game today and take full charge and responsibility of your life.

#1 - It makes your life less fulfilling as you're constantly busy functioning as a complaining machine

Playing the blame game does not end your life, but it does make it less fulfilling. Imagine you are waking up every day to only go on rants about how things or people are all doing bad things to you. What sort of person are you most likely to hang out with? The one who is cheerful and is doing great things in life or the one who is full of complaints about how things are not working out for him or her?

All of us love to hang out with people that are doers and creators, not the ones who are always whining about the huge list of their complaints all the time. If you are being that person who sounds whinful about all the bad things happening, your life will become less fulfilling. How can you ever think of enjoying the slight breeze and the fresh droplets pouring down on you, when you are so full of complain for the rain because it left you wrenched? How can you ever think about the beautiful leaves fallen on the road from the trees during the autumn when you are blaming the muddy road? Playing the blame game occupies too much mind space and keeps you from enjoying the big and little beautiful things in life. You know you deserve more than that!

#2 - Constant blame games snatch your peace of mind

When you are constantly looking for someone to shift blames onto, much of your mind space is occupied here, leaving no or less space for other things that really matter. It makes you feel frustrated towards others and this frustration shows up in different ways, say, snapping at the office boy who served you your coffee. You feel like shouting at other people around you trying to vent this frustration out. And, that snatches your peace of mind totally. It can happen every week or every day, depending on how many times you find people or circumstances to curse upon. Remember that cursing other people or things will only leave you more stressed and forever and won't do any help. All your big ambitions can go down the drain just because you are so busy being a complaint box!

#3 - Blame games make it impossible for you to change anything about you, which can totally come in the way of your own growth

When you are playing the blame game, you expect other people to change or hope your situations or circumstances will change. This expectation and hope will not let you to even consider the possibility of you changing. It will stop you from thinking that *you* need to be proactive and well prepared for all the things that happen around you.

Let's say you have a big dream of being a successful business person, but aren't able to be one. If you are into play blame games, you'll easily find a hundred reasons on why you could not be a successful business person like you never had that big business opportunity coming your way or nobody in your family has been in a big business etc. These reasons justify you not being successful with your dream of being a business person, and this justification will make you settle down with wherever you are. You will never even think about ways you could run a great business, because your mind has plenty of reasons to give you to why you're bad at it. And thus, you won't flinch a little from the place you are in. That is how many people curtail their own growth.

Here's another example. Let's say, you are striving to become more wealthy than you are now. If you stopped for a moment and asked yourself why is it that you're not being as wealthy as you want to be, what will be your answer? Do you hold yourself responsible or do you think you are showered with lots of bad luck or maybe because you weren't born and bought up in a wealthy family? Are you reasoning it out, or finding real reasons behind why it is the way it is for you?

#4 - It stops you take control of your life

Oh, you are not living in a mansion because well, your spouse isn't very rich or well, your parents didn't gift you one. These lines here will be the way of self-talk a person is likely to have who is a master champion at the game of blaming.

You will find other people and things as reasons for something bad that is happening with your own life. That way, you're giving all the powers to those external things. And this, makes you give up taking control of your life. **You will be okay with wherever you are and with whatever you are doing. And, *that* is not how you are going to be incredible!** Anything that is going wrong is happening because someone is not at their best, what more can you do about it - This is exactly how you'll begin to think. In your sub conscious mind, you've given up taking control of your life. You have given the steering of your life to other people and outer situations where in *reality*, it should be you who steers your life!

If you are the controller of your life, you will not blame other things for every bad shit that is happening in your life. Do you want to control your life? Yes? Start by taking responsibility of your life and owning everything that happens. Once you have learnt to do that, you will be surprised to know the power of immense control you can have over your life!

Learn the Art of Self-Love

Self-love is a journey that every person must embark upon at some point or another in one's life. Self-love is an act of love and kindness that is showed towards oneself and it stems from a genuine self-respect towards oneself. Self-love is an idea that says that you deserve to be loved not only by those around you but also by the most important person in your life - you! Self-love is becoming more important these days and it is definitely one of the qualities that is needed to be successful in life.

In fact, self-love goes way beyond being successful in life and it is really about feeling fulfilled by the success that comes your way. If you closely look at the lives of highly successful people, you'll see that they always uphold the principles of self-love like respecting themselves and holding a high self-esteem. Learning the art of self-love is not only confined to successful people but every person who wants great results out of life. Practicing self-love can be challenging at times due to the highs and lows of life but when learnt, it is one of the most fulfilling journeys one can ever take and it is one that leaves profound impact. So, there are no doubts that indulging and embarking upon the journey of the self-love can be highly fulfilling.

Some people misunderstand the whole concept of self-love to be one that is for narcissistic people or for the self-absorbed individuals. However, the reality is far from this myth. Self-love is not self-indulgence. Self-love is a journey of knowing ourselves better, discovering our real happiness and truly just understanding our own individual selves better. It is a journey of self-exploration and self-discover.

Self-love stems from the belief that every person deserves to be accepted and loved, first by themselves before anybody else around. Thus, decide to embark upon the journey of self-love and I can assure you that it'll be one of the most fulfilling things you'll do, leaving your soul recharged and your limiting beliefs destroyed. In this chapter, I've discussed few ways through which one can start their journey of self-love. Be prepared to feel loved, accepted, respected and pampered by the one person who'll walk with you till the end of your life - yourself.

Some simple practical ways of practicing self-love:

#1 - End the pointless comparisons you have with your peers

Like discussed in the earlier chapters, comparison is a poisonous thing to practice. There is nobody like you and thus you cannot fairly compare yourself to anybody else around you but yourself. The only person you should be comparing yourself with is you and you alone. Your previous self should be your standard to compare yourself with. How much better are you today as compared to your past self? What are the new developments and improvements you have made today to your personality that makes you better?

Ask such questions and remember that the only true Competition you have is with your old self. Not your peers at the company, not your neighbors in the street, and definitely not the celebrities you may see. It is a good habit to look upto someone and have role models in life, but you should never see them as a Competition or start comparing your life with that of theirs. Thus, stop wasting your time in these pointless comparison games and start taking action towards becoming a better version of yourself.

#2 - Invest in yourself

Investing in yourself is probably the best investment you will ever make. It is an investment that pays off ten folds more. Investing in yourself can mean investing both your time and energy into building your personality and skillsets, both all the same. Sign up for those courses that you know will make you better at something you've always wanted to work on. Invest time into learning new things. Depending on what you do, there are always a bunch of new skills that you can learn and master. Invest there and you'll feel much refreshed and energized by these.

#3 - Indulge in physical activities

Exercising is important. We have heard this all our lives and yet most of us do not take working out or exercising seriously. Physical activities are very important to keep up our health and they're also very good for our mental and emotional well-being. Sign up for those beginner work-out classes if you want to start small. Remember that your physical fitness will come a long way in ensuring your overall health. Stay fit by regularly indulging in fitness activities. A nice body will also give you lots of confidence from within which will not only make you fall in love with yourself, but makes others like you too. A physically fit person is always very positive and attractive.

#4 - Be mindful of the things you consume, what you eat and what you think/read

Being mindful of what you consume is an inseparable part of self-love journey. What you eat defines the physical fitness of your body. Similarly, the thoughts that you consume are equally important. Reading depressing and negative news all day along will give you a negative outlook of life, which is unhealthy for you. Just like you are aware of what diets to follow to be healthy, being mindful of what kind of thoughts you consume is extremely important too. Don't waste your time in reading about or talking to people who discuss the unnecessary gossips. Instead, indulge in thoughtful conversations with the people around you and you'll be surprised how motivated and positive that'll keep you all day along.

#5 - End all the toxic relationships in your life

Whether we admit it or not, many of us are trapped in some kind of toxic relationships. It can be with friends or someone in your family. Toxic relationships undermine your self-respect and hamper your personal growth. There is no need for any kind of negativity in your life and thus, for your own good, it is best to recognize the toxic relationships of your life and make attempts to end them. There is no meaning to life when you have surrounded yourself with people who make you feel like you're like nothing. Your inner circle is very important in determining your success and thus, pluck out all the toxic relationships from your life.

#6 - Get out of your comfort zone every now and then, and try new things

Getting out of your comfort zone makes you understand yourself better in a way that will uplift you. You will discover the new boundaries that you have and you might realize that you're very talented at something you never realized before. Make it a habit to actively get out of your comfort zone every now and then. Don't be afraid to try new things, from hobbies to interests to passions. There is certainly a beauty in the fleeting passions and you might just discover a hidden talent that brings you much joy and happiness.

#7 - Celebrate your wins, the big and the small

Celebrating your little wins along the way is what makes success and victory worthwhile. Don't shy away from accepting compliments and don't be afraid to celebrate the little wins you may have on your way. Celebrate them in all its glory and give yourself credit for making it this far. Regardless how small an achievement may seem, make it a point to celebrate it and you'll notice how that will only push you further towards achieving your bigger goals.